The Million $ Rainmaker

A Parable
About
Developing
New Business

The Million $ Rainmaker

A Parable
About
Developing New Business

By Ed Robinson

Published by
Advanced Marketing Concepts, Inc.
San Antonio, TX   78248
www.Edspeaks.com
1-800-381-1433

Printed in the United States of America
ISBN 0-9745289-1-9 $19.85

Forward By John Alston

Ed Robinson has written a delightful, colorfully vivid and well-crafted parable that takes any aspiring Rainmaker on an instructive journey. Within the body of this parable, are embedded tools and strategies for developing new business.

What is a Rainmaker?

A Rainmaker, according to Jeffrey J. Fox's description of the Native American tradition, uses "...magical powers to bring rain to nourish the crops to feed the people who would weaken, die, or have to move elsewhere." In a business, a Rainmaker is a person who brings revenue into an organization...." A Rainmaker is a person who knows what to do to make prosperity happen. What should you do to develop new business? The answer is here.

From the moment of conception, "life" beckons us to unfold, expand, come forth, and find our "meant to be." Obviously, physical growth occurs just as a part of the natural scheme of things; it's life's natural design. Then there is conscious, emotional, psychological, and normal developmental growth that occurs as a result of how we mindfully meet and respond to daily challenges. In the world of work, and/or running a business, we are exposed to a multitude of contingencies with all sorts of challenges. It is from these challenges that growth is initiated in business and pursued by each one of us, in our need to gain wisdom.

In "The Million $ Rainmaker," one learns what growth steps to take to develop new business. These steps are consistent with enduring principles and strategies that enable one to respond to business realities!

Herein, we're reminded that it's our actions that count and our actions have consequences. The question of all questions is, "What actions should I take...What should I do to develop new business?" Well, again, the answers are here. Herein are insights that come through the people who've benefited from challenges in business. They are people who have become Rainmakers or are on their way to becoming one. The exchange of ideas, the sharing of experiences and the wisdom derived from their respective challenges, become tools to use and strategies to practice in new business development. This parable, is expressed from within the context of a diverse and changing world. A world where, regardless of the challenge you face, life goes on, and the only way out is through. What you do depends on what you learn to do.

Ed Robinson has written this parable for those who have rich aspirations, are striving to prosper, profit and benefit from having applied the Rainmaker's knowledge. In this parable, the visionaries and achievers bring unique powerful lessons to the reader, and specify the actions required for new business development.

Ed Robinson, has taken the best of what he has learned, through his coaching and consulting practice, and woven it into the story of a person participating successfully in business who suddenly hits the wall. It's here, like with all of us, where fear, and frustration lead to the quest for solutions and answers. For those who want a robust and prosperous experience, they will remember that it's the actions in which we engage that enable us to develop new business. This book offers a powerful and meaningful reminder as to what is demanded and what works to achieve the goal of becoming a Rainmaker.

Dedication

To all of my Heroes, Sheroes, Coaches
and Mentors for being beacons and
Benjamins in my life. Your constant influence
propels me to move beyond my dreams and desires.

To my pillars of strength: Jo, Alex, Steven, Eddie,
Louise, Jack, Tristan and Trace and
the Good Lord for Blessing me with
each and every one of you.

Acknowledgements

First and foremost, to my consulting clients around the world, thank you. You had the faith to give me the opportunity to work with you, explore new territories and even experiment to discover new processes even when they challenged your norms. Thanks for having faith in the processes and giving me encouragement to keep thinking and working with you.

I must acknowledge the wisdom, careful eye and loving heart of my cheerful companion Jo (Joann) for putting up with my crazy schedule, hectic life and Me in general. Thanks for being my life companion and for keeping a smile on my face and in my heart. Thanks also for editing every word I write and making sure I look good on paper.

Speaking of editing, in addition to Jo, I'd like to thank Darlena Campbell for editing and providing a scrupulous eye on this long and wonderful ride.

Next I need to express great appreciation to Laura Baker for editing, coaching and making sure I stayed focus. Your mark and touch is woven throughout this entire book.

Finally, I am grateful to my business coaches both formal and informal, for sculpting the professional I've become.

Special mention to Walter Haley, Mark LeBlanc, Steve Straus, Richard Terrell, Ron Willingham and Roy Terracina, for your wisdom over the years has shaped and guided me. Thank You.

66

In the end, it's whether or not you really care about these people you want to be your clients that allows you to make that sweet rain. Like music, finding that right rhythm with a potential client is when the rain finally comes your way.

99

~ Benjamin

Contents

Contents

"

Now he was facing the toughest transition of his life. To make partner, he had to bring in new clients and lots of them.

"

Chapter 1

The Search for Guidance

From outside, looking into the plate-glass office, the Senior Manager of a medium-sized accounting and consulting firm looked like he had it all. After five years with the firm, he had shown incredible skill in service management. His implementation processes were impeccable. Junior and senior accountants alike looked to the Senior Manager for inspiration and guidance. His project teams had even earned awards in the industry.

Looking out at the bustling office around him, the Senior Manager tried to dismiss the nagging feeling in the pit of his stomach that there were still parts of this business where he felt that he didn't know what he was doing.

Just last night, he had once again attended a private networking dinner on the estate of a good friend. As the cocktails were poured and the courses served, the

Senior Manager found himself casting about for topics of conversation that would somehow lead to a dialogue around new business opportunities with his firm. That conversation had never happened for him and it failed to happen again last night. He left feeling nothing less than inept.

It hadn't been easy going from a first year kid right out of school up to Senior Manager in just five years. He'd watched a lot of his peers leave from exhaustion, discouragement or alternative career choices. He realized now that when it came to accounting practices and project management, he had known what to do instinctively. Numbers, systems, equations all came automatically to him. Now he was facing the toughest transition of his life. To make partner, he had to bring in new clients and lots of them. The Senior Manager checked his watch. It was six P.M., time to go home. His shoulders sagged slightly as he packed up his briefcase. For the first time in a long time, since he had tried out for the high school musical, the Senior Manager felt truly confused and out-of-place.

He'd done well…well enough. His new bride was happy. She was so great: Rozlyn. It had been Rozlyn's idea that they join a foundation devoted to serving the inner-city schools. They had only begun their involvement and already he had met some of the most influential and motivated people imaginable.

He had many reasons to feel proud but taking the elevator down, the Senior Manager knew in his gut that his arid sales record made him a failure. For him, failure was not an option. He *had* to become more fluent in client development; he had to become a Rainmaker.

As he slipped the key into the driver side door of his BMW, the Senior Manager slipped his hand into his coat pocket and pulled out his cell phone. Before he started the engine, he dialed his sister's number.

A top partner in one of the largest law firms on the west coast, he expected her to be behind her desk. Instead, he heard the clinking of many dishes when she answered. Her voice came to him warmly. "Hey Eugene! What's up? Let me step outside so I can

3

hear!" He realized that his sister was at her volunteer position as a server in a home for the elderly.

"Hey Sis…" Within a few minutes, Eugene had spilled his worries about his lack of sales abilities to his sister. She listened empathetically but made no suggestions. Finally, he paused and waited silently. He wasn't going to beg for her advice, but he sure could use it right now. He knew that his sister routinely landed high profile clients for her firm and he had even been with her when new clients had called *her* and asked to retain her services. She must know a secret he didn't. His sister grew quiet on her end as well. He could hear faint laughter and singing in the distance. Finally, she spoke,

"I'm so sorry to hear that. Do you have a pen?"

"Yes."

"Take down this address." She gave him directions to an address located outside of the city in a remote area. "Go to see Benjamin and tell him I sent you." She paused. "That's all I can tell you Little Brother. I've

4

been waiting for you to bring this up. I want to point you in the right direction."

He didn't know what to say. "OK., I guess," he agreed begrudgingly.

"Gotta go! Love ya!" She called out and the line beeped off.

It was growing dark in the company parking lot. Only a few cars were left. Oddly shaken, Eugene's brain struggled to categorize his conversation with his sister. No amount of linear thinking would explain to him her unusual refusal to help him and her strange insistence that he drive to an address outside of town.

Eugene folded up the address and sat still in his car, his keys idle in his lap.

He had always relied on his gut instincts when everything else failed.

"What do I have to lose?" he asked himself. He turned the key in the ignition and as the purr of the

"Beamer" enveloped him, he shifted into first gear and pulled away. The competitor in him rose to the challenge. "Benjamin, it looks like we're going to meet." The beginnings of a smile played around the corners of his mouth.

"

He had always relied on his gut instincts when everything else failed.

"

"

He winked at Eugene. "We trust each other. She knows that I won't hurt her, so," he grinned, "she does not crush me."

"

Chapter 2

Commit to a Journey and
Enjoy the Ride

The next morning, Eugene cleared his schedule, told
his executive assistant and his second-in-command
that he would be gone the rest of the day and he set
out north of town where unbroken prairie stretched
for hundreds of miles in all directions. He followed
his sister's instructions and after a couple of hours,
found himself pulling up to the gateway of an impres-
sive ranch.

He had only driven a few hundred yards onto the
property when he saw a black stallion galloping
toward him. It was a ranch and this was cowboy
country, but it was hardly the controlled business
etiquette to which he was accustomed. The magnifi-
cent horse came to a standstill right in front of his car
and he slammed on the brakes. "What the?!!"

9

The rider dismounted gracefully and he saw that it was a woman, an Asian woman with short gray hair. Her gaze was inscrutable.

"How can I help you?"

"I came to see Benjamin," he said trying to take an official tone. Her eyes locked onto his.

"Do you have an appointment?" she asked.

He shook his head, "No. I was told I didn't really need one."

"Who sent you?" she pressed.

Eugene felt himself start to sweat. What sort of place was this? He gave the woman his sister's name. She nodded and said, "Oh yes. Follow me."

For another two miles he drove behind the great stallion to the entrance of a stone mansion, sprawling out in granite and stucco verandas, courtyards and beautiful tiled roofs.

A dark young man opened his car door gracefully. "Come with me," he instructed with a strong British accent. Eugene followed the young man past carved doors down a pink granite walkway shaded by vines that blocked the beating sun. They walked through a courtyard and into a tree-covered area leading to a corral. Three barns circled the corral and in the center pranced four or five high-spirited Arabian horses kicking up their heels and nipping one another. An elderly man wearing a khaki shirt and blue jeans stepped out from the farthest barn and began to walk toward him. As the old man approached the playful horses, he spoke to them in a low gentle voice. Almost immediately the horses subsided and formed a line facing him. He paused before each one and spoke to them scratching the area just behind their right ear. When he reached the gate where Eugene stood, the old man gave a short whistle and horses broke rank and began their frolicking again.

"How can I help you?" The weathered fellow asked in a slightly clipped accent that Eugene could not place.

"I'm here to see Benjamin." Eugene called. "Has he gone riding?"

The fellow smiled and without saying a word walked over to a massive roan tethered near the gate. Her flanks were covered in dust and sweat. He handed Eugene a large flat brush. "Sophie needs to be brushed. Will you help me?"

Without waiting for an answer, the old man ducked under the roan's neck and began brushing her right side with long, gentle strokes.

Eugene felt his blood begin to boil. "No offence, sir, but I've come a long way to see Benjamin, not to groom horses."

At that moment, the young man who had greeted him reappeared. "Excuse me, Mr. Benjamin, Sir, your lunch is ready."

"Thank you, Shibu," he replied with a smile. "We'll be there shortly." Eugene felt his face grow intensely warm.

"I apologize, Sir. I did not realize..," his voice trailed off. Benjamin smiled at him and continued brushing the flanks of the roan.

"Just lend a hand here." As he spoke, the roan began to toss her head and step sideways on her tether. Benjamin placed his hand firmly against her rump and pressed down persistently with his fingers until she returned to the right position. He winked at the younger man. "We trust each other. She knows that I won't hurt her, so," he grinned, "she does not crush me."

They brushed the horse in silence; Eugene's mind slowly stopped its frantic racing and fell into the rhythm of the horse's breath. The dank smell from her body and her warmth permeated him through his fingers. He found his left hand following the brush in a gentle rhythm after each stroke. He could feel her muscles ripple under his hand.

As they put away the brushes and let the roan out to pasture, Benjamin mused, "You know it's not unlike a bank, the trust we develop with an animal, or with

13

people for that matter." Eugene returned a blank stare.

"I'm sorry?"

"What I mean to say," Benjamin explained, "is that each time I touch and work with a horse I'm making a deposit into their trust account, so-to-speak. Once the balance is high enough, we have what I like to call a 'working trust.' That means that we can both let down our guard and work together." He paused reflectively, "It does take time and considerable effort as well as a great level of genuineness. It would be a lot easier for me to let one of my staff groom the horses that I ride, but then I might find myself with a horse that has no trust in me when I need it the most." Eugene nodded, slowly making the connection to customers, though the whole concept was still foggy in his mind.

A short while later, he followed Benjamin into an elaborate changing room, where he was given a set of new clothes and fine tooled boots that fit perfectly. They sat down to eat on a large balcony overlooking an interior courtyard. In the courtyard stood a fountain made with the most beautiful mosaic tiles Eugene had ever seen. Shibu served them a sumptuous meal of exotic dishes. Benjamin ate with great enjoyment.

"It's good, if I do say so myself." He laid down his fork. "My staff consists of handpicked people from around the world. I like to surround myself with people who are initially very unfamiliar to me. Each week, I take a cooking lesson from my chef. I seek out opportunities to ask for advice and information. Yes, even at my age, it's still personally rewarding to constantly be learning! There are so many things I do not know. And," he added with a twinkle in his eye, "I remember that there was one thing that I desperately needed to know when I was a Senior Manager. I had so many responsibilities. I had a lot of things to juggle and I also had to develop new clients."

"I started out as a staff consultant right out of college. I made it to Senior after two years and then Manager. After I hit Senior I kind of topped out or plateaued for longer than I liked. I was lost without a map. Every attempt I made to woo a new client flopped. That's when I realized that I needed outside help. I asked for what I needed and a mentor introduced me to a coach, *my* Benjamin. He taught me the secret of transforming prospects into relationships and relationships into clients, allowing me to continue my journey to become a Rainmaker. I promised to pass that secret on and to mentor those who came to me for advice. I met your sister not too many years ago. She truly is an excellent seeker of knowledge."

Benjamin stood up and looked around him with satisfaction. "Years ago I stopped counting my clients. Today we work with each other now, in a sense." He looked over at his guest. "How may clients have you brought in this year?" Eugene swallowed hard.

"None."

"Why is that? Why is it that someone who has met the challenges of leading people and mastering today's technological developments has not had the same success in client development?"

Eugene shrugged. "I'm ....I guess I'm missing

something…some part of the puzzle or something."

Benjamin leaned back against the balcony railing. "You know, Son, riding horses scared the hell out of me at first. It was new, even foreign to me. Once I learned how to make a connection with my horse, I realized that my horse knew intuitively the direction to go." He glanced knowingly at Eugene, "Are you telling me that you need to learn something new?"

Not being accustomed to sharing a weakness in his professionalism, Eugene thought to himself "Hmm, I guess I do need to learn a new skill." He sighed, "Yes. I know that it shouldn't be as difficult as it is."

Benjamin nodded. "Are you ready to start now?"

Eugene focused his gaze on the setting sun outside. He let his mind go over the events of the last couple of days. He brought to his mind the frustration that had been building in him whenever he attempted to win a new client. He recalled his sister and her success and her love for him. He looked around him at Benjamin's wealth, mastery and sagaciousness. He knew that he wanted the same wealth and mastery for himself. He took a deep breath and said more firmly, "Yes, I am ready."

"

Why is it that someone who has met the challenges of leading people and mastering today's techno-logical developments has not had the same success in client development?

"

"

I learned long ago that the more I could discipline myself to develop relationships with people I did not seem to have much in common with at first glance, the broader my understanding of clients would be and the more I could serve all clients.

"

Chapter 3

Risk, Discomfort and Fear

"Very well, " Benjamin said. "I suggest that you make whatever arrangements you need to make to stay here a couple more days."

Eugene's eyes opened wide in surprise. "I didn't realize…My staff…meetings."

Benjamin turned briskly toward the stairway, waving him along. "Let me introduce you to my staff." They walked together down into the tiled courtyard. The sound of laughing and talking voices quieted down as they entered. As they walked around the courtyard, Benjamin introduced Eugene to each of his staff. "This is Yi. She is in charge of the house electronics. This is Born; he is my hardware/software support person. This is Magla: She is the veterinarian who cares for the mares. Magla is from Indonesia. This is Toshi: he is security." With each new face and name,

Eugene came into contact with a different language and culture. Benjamin saw his surprise. "I learned long ago that the more I could discipline myself to develop relationships with people I did not seem to have much in common with at first glance, the broader my understanding of clients would be and the more I could serve all clients."

He smiled, "As a matter-of-fact, I brought in multi-million dollar clients into my company from so many diverse backgrounds and cultures they nicknamed me 'UN'." He chuckled. "I have since continued to stretch myself even though I no longer need to bring in new clients. I sold my former firm as well as several others, but I now look forward to the challenge of pushing through the discomfort of difference to find common ground."

Eugene felt his anxiety rising. What was he doing here? Could he really learn an entirely new way of being in just a few days? Was he crazy? Was Benjamin? He knew that he wanted a sage, a mentor and coach. He blurted out, "So, is *that* the secret?"

Benjamin paused at the foot of an ornate spiral staircase, "Yes, that is one part of the secret, of the equation, if you will, to becoming a Rainmaker. Another part of the equation is to ask what you can do for your prospective client, *not* what they can do for you. I'm sure that you know that sometimes the best thing you can do for someone is just to listen to them, but did you know that that is a key for you, or anyone, to transform into a Rainmaker?"

He continued talking as he climbed the stairs. "I remember sitting in the Commodore Club at the airport (a room reserved for high-end corporate clients). I was sipping a cup of coffee and reading a book when an elderly woman wearing sensible shoes and carrying a cat cage sat down near me. After awhile, I inquired as to her cat's name. She told me that it was Captain Boots. 'I outrank him,' she said and I laughed without realizing to what she was alluding. I asked her a few more questions about Captain Boots. She answered eagerly. She must have spoken to me for thirty minutes about her cat and his difficulty with flying, his recent operation etc. I could tell she was feeling anxious about her pet as well as

23

the impending flight, so I tried to give her my attention and empathy, though the truth is that I'm a dog/horse person myself. Eventually, my flight was boarding and I rose to leave."

" 'You are a nice person,' she told me with an air of authority. 'Do you have a card?' It was when I stood up and handed her my card that I noticed she wore the insignia of a U.S. Navy Admiral on her lapel. To make a long story short, my friend, that Admiral was my first multimillion-dollar client to bring into my firm. She owned a number of shopping malls and car rental agencies. My former accounting firm still oversees all of her holdings. That experience as well as my work with horses proved what *my* Benjamin taught me. The only way to earn someone's business is to earn their trust and the best way to earn their trust is to simply be attentive to them."

He looked out the upstairs French doors that faced the corral. "I brush and clean the hooves of my personal riding horses myself. Horses are prey animals and humans are predators, so horses are naturally wary. I need my horses to remember me and to trust me, my life depends on it, so, I touch them frequently. Actually," he winked, "touching is part of the equation. I'll share it with you later."

As Benjamin spoke, he was leading Eugene down a hallway and past many rooms. The Senior Manager caught sight of opulent beds with satin covers, carved armchairs, plush carpets of every kind, small theaters, hot tubs, technology stations and wet bars. His step lightened in anticipation. If he was going to leave his office for a few days, he might as well enjoy himself.

"Here is your room, " Benjamin pushed open a narrow door.

Eugene stepped inside and his heart sank in dismay. In a rising panic he turned to Benjamin. "Are you sure that this is my room?"

Benjamin looked at his guest's pleading eyes and nodded firmly. "Yes." He then handed Eugene a folded piece of paper. "This is a complete list of the staff's names, areas of responsibility and phone numbers. The room is sparse, but you can speak to any one of my staff if you wish for something. They will be happy to help you." With that, Benjamin excused himself and left the dumbfounded man standing in the middle of a small room that was completely empty except for a bare mattress on a metal frame and a telephone. The one window looked out onto a concrete wall only five or six feet away.

He sank heavily onto the bed and let his head fall into his hands. What had he done?Eugene sat motionless thinking random thoughts. He decided finally, to leave. This was too strange, too bizarre: black stallions, foreign staff, secrets, a long line of Benjamins and now this pathetic cell of a room…What had his sister meant by sending him here? "There has to be a book I can read on my own about what it takes to develop a client base," he told himself without conviction. Dispiritedly, he put his hand on the knob and tried to twist it. The knob would not move. He realized that Benjamin had locked the door behind him.

"

Another part of the equation is to ask what you can do for your prospective client, not what they can do for you.

"

"

The only way to earn someone's business is to earn their trust and the best way to earn their trust is to simply be attentive to them.

"

28

Chapter 4

Listen, Focus and Connect

Eugene took his hand away from the knob. He wasn't surprised that the door was locked, that was part of the challenge wasn't it? His competitive spirit rose to the surface as it often did – a
survival instinct that had landed him in this time and place, this threshold. He turned toward the wall outside his window, his mind clicking furiously to develop a strategy and untangle the puzzle of his imprisonment. He pondered a second, wondering if the imprisonment was real or mental.

Eugene had long ago disciplined himself to focus on what he *did* want in clear detail, avoiding all thoughts of what he did not want. He remembered too that in life there are circumstances he controlled and influenced as well as those he had no control over. He immediately shifted his thinking to what, in this moment, he could control or influence.

He stood very still now taking his imagination step-by-step over what he truly wanted. First, he wanted a room as luxurious as any of those he had passed in the hall. He created a picture in his mind of this room; inserting a technology station, voluptuous carpeting and bedding, a hot tub and a large-screen plasma TV. He then pictured himself in a similar room and house that belonged to him and a roster of large clients at his fingertips. Feeling buzzed from his self-induced sense of success, Eugene sat down on the bed and glanced at the list Benjamin had left for him. " Let's do this!" He summoned his inner forces.

Without waiting to second-guess himself, he grabbed the receiver, surprised to see that the phone was a rotary style. The first number he dialed was that of Shibu, the House Manager. He had had more contact with Shibu than anyone else, so why not start with him? Eugene let the phone ring eleven times before he hung up. No answer. He began immediately to dial Toshi's number. As a Senior Manager, he had traveled to Japan twice. He felt confident that he could sustain a conversation with Toshi. To his amazement, Toshi's phone also rang over eleven times. Eugene dropped the receiver back on its cradle. He put his fingers in the dial and waited as each number rolled around: He would not stop! He would find at least one person to talk to if he had to call every number! Half an hour later, Eugene rested his right hand on his knee. Not one single line had picked up – not even an answering machine, let alone a voice mail message!

Exasperated, he stretched out on the bare mattress and closed his eyes. He had nothing – the familiar accounting sign for nothing, a zero with a line through it crossed his mind. In a flash, he sat up in bed. No! He didn't have null, he had zero! Thinking about the theorem of infinity, Eugene turned the paper over. On the back, at the top of the page was a single listing: Val Scholoss – operator – 0. Val? What country could that be? Then he racked his brain for tidbits on the Baltic, or Russia or Germany. He felt strangely alive and his heart was racing with anxiety and adrenaline. He dialed zero.

The phone rang once and then a nasally female voice came on the line. "This is Val. How can I help you?" She had an accent, a thick accent from up in the northeastern part of the U.S. somewhere. His brain scrambled to place it while he stalled for time, "Oh, hi Val. This is Eugene. I'm a guest…" She cut him off politely,

"Yes, Sir." A silence drew out between them for three seconds. He started again,

"I…I can't place your accent Val. Is that Brooklyn?"

"Na. I'm from Jersey: Red Bank, New Jersey, but that's not a bad guess." Eugene blinked. Jersey? All he knew about New Jersey was that the license plate said, "Garden State."

"Really? Red Bank? You…you know I don't know a thing about New Jersey. I've never even been there." He paused. "What's it like?"

"Jersey?" Val gave a short laugh. He tried to picture her in his mind. When he had met everyone in the

32

courtyard earlier he seemed to remember a young woman wearing a bright pink sweater with big buttons, tight jeans and heels. Her hair had been long, curly with red highlights. "Jersey's not bad. It's got its pretty places, even mountains. Where I lived, Red Bank, was a fun place." Val rambled on and Eugene felt his body ease back against the wall. For a second, he tuned out, and then he realized that he wasn't paying attention to her when he heard her say, "…monster trucks."

He sat up. "I'm sorry, did you say monster trucks?"

"Yeah, Gus, my husband, we just got married, he has a monster truck arena. You know, like for bull fighting or baseball, 'cept for monster trucks."

Eugene's wife had recently suggested to him that he learn the game of golf so that he could join the new country club and play the new course everyone was talking about. He felt the air leave his lungs. His mind went blank. Here was the only person in this "castle" to answer his call and she was far more foreign to him than anyone else could possibly be: a woman, a young woman from Jersey with a husband in the monster truck business.

"Hmmm. You…you know, Val, I'm a novice when it comes to…" he stumbled, he cleared his throat, "…to both marriage and monster trucks. Yeah! That's right. I just got married too! I guess we're both newlyweds."

"Ohooo!" Val let out a purely feminine squeal of camaraderie. "What d'ya know about that? When did you tie the knot?"

"In August, the fifth." Again, a squeal of ecstasy.

"NO KIDDING!! I got married in August too, the nineteenth!!" Eugene couldn't believe his good luck as Val stumbled over herself to tell him about her recent wedding. While he was married to a woman and he *did* have an older sister, Eugene had never really understood the way that women could generate high-pitched excitement between themselves so easily. Now, he realized, it was simply about sharing emotions and the excitement of connecting. For half

an hour, he and Val exchanged wedding memories
and he began to miss Rozlyn very much. "So,
Eugene, we've been talking a mile a minute. I forgot
to ask you where you want to go."

Eugene stammered, "Go?"

"You know, who did you want to talk to?"

"Oh, uh well…Shibu. I did call his number, but no
one picked up."

"Yeah that's about right! That's because it's his day
off. He's going to be in his quarters. You'll jus' have
to go over there, 'cause he doesn't answer phones on
his day off. Oh, gotta go. Talk to you soon, Eugene!"
Val's line clicked off.

Eugene stood up. He felt lighthearted– as if he'd just
gone for a long walk or had a massage. Reliving his
wedding with Val had been a nice experience for him.
He realized that he hadn't spoken to anyone, not even
Rozlyn about his feelings during the ceremony. He
also realized that his new state of mind had to do with

the conversation he'd had with Val. "I made a connection and I got what I asked for, a way to talk to Shibu."

In his new boots, Eugene walked across the plank floor. He turned the doorknob and much to his surprise, the door opened. He walked into the hallway. At the end of the hallway, near the stairwell sat Benjamin in a brown easy chair reading. As Eugene approached him, he looked up. "You have learned many lessons already." He glanced back down at his book absently. "Val has constant access to everyone here. Did you tell her what you wanted? Did you ask her to be an advocate for you?" He tried to rise, "Here, give me a hand, will you?"

Still a little steamed about his accommodations, Eugene realized that his personal comfort wasn't his key purpose for being here. He gently pulled the oldman out of the big chair, surprised. He was as light as a feather. "An advocate?"

"Yes, an advocate is someone who knows you and will help you open doors to others. An advocate can be a gatekeeper. For instance, Val is a gatekeeper. Through her, you could make many connections."

"No," Eugene finally answered his question, "I didn't ask her to be an advocate for me." He made a mental note to do so. Why hadn't he even considered that as a possibility?

"You are more likely to get what you seek if you ask for it, once you've established a connection that is." They descended the stairs slowly. "Let me show you the way to Shibu's cottage."

Eugene started. How did Benjamin know that he wanted Shibu?

As they walked through the great rooms of the house, Benjamin stopped before a large round mirror and smiled at his own reflection. "An old South African once told me something I'll never forget. I was a young man like you at the time, seeking the secrets to developing business. He told me to look out the window. We were near a busy market and I could see it was full of vendors and buyers. I told him what I saw. Then, he held up a mirror and instructed me to look into it. 'Now, what do you see?' he said. 'I see my own reflection,' I told him, feeling a bit silly. 'That,' he said, 'is what happens when you let silver get between you and the market.'" Benjamin's old brown eyes locked onto Eugene's for a moment then he chuckled, grinned a little and resumed his progress toward the back of the house.

"

...an advocate is someone who knows you and will help you open doors to others. An advocate can be a gatekeeper.

"

"

*You are more likely to get
what you seek if you ask
for it, once you've
established a connection
that is.*

"

Chapter 5

A Quest for Success

"When you're ready, Eugene, Shibu stays in the cottage just behind the foal pasture." Benjamin led the way into the middle barn. Inside the tack room, the two men stood on a raised wooden platform that held a refrigerator full of carrots as well as a series of saddles, a pile of blankets, harnesses and bridles, work gloves, spare hats and an old blackboard where medications and riding schedules were listed in neat columns. Twenty yards away in the barn they caught sight of Magla, the veterinarian, standing before a grouping of grain bins with a scoop in her hand. Two colts nuzzled two white Arabian mares with black markings in the stalls behind her. "Benjamin called out, "How are our two newborns?"

"Luna is standing longer now. Estrella has even started running a bit!" she called out with motherly pride.

41

"Magla is such an incredible and unusual scientist," Benjamin said to Eugene as they turned to go. She has the best technical understanding of equine biology I have ever come across: the chemistry, physics, all of it, yet she 'listens' for lack of a better word, to the horses' own language. She has remarkable intuition. I would say that her technical experience supports her intuition; it never supersedes it. It's similar to client development, Eugene. Your technical ability needs to be tied to intuition if you're going to help others."

Benjamin glanced around and grabbed a piece of chalk, "Do you enjoy equations? Let me show you the one that has been my model for success and balance for years now." In a blank space on the blackboard he wrote,

$$(TA + CRS + PA) \times AD = Success$$

"This is technical ability plus customer relationship skills, plus persuasive ability. Take the sum of these and multiply it by what I refer to as the leverage factor, your achievement drive and that will equal success…provided your variables have high values, of course." Benjamin looked at what he had written, "Let me further define this equation, " he said. "Technical Ability (TA) is having the competency to carry out the processes, the skills and knowledge, the necessary regulations and the policies. It also means knowing how to come to the conclusions that give you a complete work product."

"Now, Client Relationship Skills (CRS) are also a set of competencies formulated into a process, a defined process, that we can hold as a future lesson for us. CRS is the ability to focus on the people we serve, our customers, both internal and external customers. Years ago, people would go through professional service firms and have the technical competency to be a specialist. With only that TA they would be promoted up the ladder only to be stifled at some point with the realization that more was needed to be in a leadership position. Today if people, specifically managers like you, do not develop these other skills they become stuck in those positions for life. These professionals would never make that quantum leap from Manager to Partner or Director. Can you see how it is imperative to not only have technical ability,

but also client relationship skills as well?" Eugene
nodded, soaking it all in.

Benjamin pointed to the PA part of the equation.
"Persuasive Ability gets other people to follow our
lead, to believe in our ideas. Realize though, that
what this boils down to is your written and oral
communication style."

"We finally sum all of these, and multiply them by
our leverage factor which is AD or your achievement
drive. Eugene, what do you think achievement drive
is all about?" Eugene smiled, this was what he
considered to be his "sweet spot", he expounded
saying "I think achievement drive is your own
motivation, desire and incentive to do what you do in
life.' Benjamin smiled "Well put!" He continued.
"The first three variables are objective, they are
defined processes. A person could lack in these traits,
yet if they are cognizant of that shortcoming, they
could learn each of them." Then, in a firm tone he
added, "AD is subjective to your desire. It determines

how well and how high you can achieve in anything in life."

Eugene stared at the equation as Benjamin wandered back toward the newborn colts. He was starting to get it and he began to give his personal values to each of the variables. Eugene was very confident in his abilities yet realistic when it came to growth. He gave himself an 8 on a scale of 1 to 10, with 10 being the highest. As he started piecing things together Eugene thought, "Now we are gaining some traction!"

"

...he held up a mirror and instructed me to look into it. 'Now, what do you see?' he said. 'I see my own reflection,' I told him, feeling a bit silly. 'That,' he said, 'is what happens when you let silver get between you and the market.'

"

Chapter 6

Persistence Rules

Eugene blinked rapidly, still taking a personal inventory. He knew that his technical competency was strong and the achievement drive, well, he had no problem with that either. His persuasive ability and customer relationship skills needed work. He glanced nervously toward Benjamin and thought. "Ask for what you want, learn to learn," he reminded himself. "Uh, Benjamin, is there any *other* formula? Perhaps one that address the CRS and PA in particular?"

The old man looked pleased and grinned broadly, "No, my friend, there's no formula, magic wand or potion in the world except this." He pointed to his heart. "You've got to follow your heart, your gut, your intuition, your inner...whatever you want to call it." He tilted his head in Magla's direction. "Everyday she walks among the pregnant mares, touching each one and letting the mare touch her, breathe and move around her. They are as expressive as neon signs if you stand still." He paused and repeated quietly, almost to himself, "Stand still and listen with your ears and eyes."

They stood in the barn for almost a minute without speaking. Eugene realized with surprise that he was in no hurry. He felt like he could stand quietly in the barn listening to the clanking doors, whinnies and muffled voices indefinitely. Benjamin picked up the chalk again, "There is a formula I use to manage time in my marketing efforts. Just like you manage projects and people it's important to carve specific time to develop clients on purpose. By *on purpose* I mean to take a proactive approach to growing business as opposed to merely hoping it will happen." Below the first equation he wrote,

$$\{ \ (80/20) \ 16 \ (m^3) \ \}$$

"Eighty percent of your income will come from twenty percent of your clients. Eighty percent of your results come from twenty percent of your efforts.

"Eighty percent of your potential clients will come from twenty percent of the people that you know and that know you. Remember us talking about advocates? Put together a list of about 25 potential advocates. They can be referral sources, targeted clients or even people who just appreciate the efforts you put forth in the work that you do. The sixteen is the number of times you need to 'touch' that is, make some form of contact with your advocates each year. Most people will quit interfacing with clients after five times. The fact is that after five times, only twenty percent of the people will make a decision about you and your services. But if you make a persistent systematic effort to touch them sixteen times the percentage goes up to about seventy percent depending on the quality of your list.

I always contacted my advocates, either by mail, phone, email or even sending them an article or something that may be of interest to them every month. That gave me twelve touches each year. Then I would make an effort to take two people a week to lunch, coffee or an event. By focusing on two per week I would go through my list of 25 once a quarter allowing for four more significant contacts each year for a total of 16. With this system, around seventy percent buy because you've made those significant touches. Remember when we were grooming the horse? Touching means sincerity and connection, in other words, enhancing the level of trust.

The m^3 refers to a mastermind-mentoring group. You need to have support and encouragement from people who have similar goals. These people will push you to do the level of research you need to do before you contact a potential client. It's hard to break the ice and nothing increases your confidence level better than knowing a lot about a person and their company. Mastermind groups keep you learning about business, people and yourself which in turn boosts your confidence so much that…well, you're hard to resist. Then you feed off of each other's energy creating lasting bonds."

Eugene quickly memorized the equations. This "touching" idea might be doable and he certainly knew how to research a subject. Eugene's mind opened to the possibility that, with these tools, he could become comfortable, skilled and even masterful at attracting and keeping clients. A muscle inside of his neck released and he smiled; an irrepressible boyish glee came over him. He laughed to himself and whispered, "Here we go!

"

{　(80/20) 16 (m^3)　}

"

52

Chapter 7

Put Yourself in New Situations

Benjamin squinted in the sunlight and pointed to a stand of pecan trees. "You see those trees? Take a sharp left when you reach them and follow the trail by the river about half a mile. You'll see Shibu's house. It's the first one you come to." Eugene thanked Benjamin and set out, already wondering at Shibu's lifestyle choices. He figured that the House Manager of such a large operation could certainly afford to live off-site. He thought of his own tri-level condo with its white stucco and white carpeting. It had the insulated feel of black leather and glass. Rozlyn had brought a few things with her when they married, but neither of them had had the time to redecorate.

The walk was hot, but pleasant. Eugene was grateful for the old straw hat Benjamin had shoved on his head. When he reached the pecan trees, he stood in the shade and watched the river for a minute. Being at the estate had heightened his sense of enjoying the moment. Eugene had only gone a short distance when he saw ahead of him a charming cottage built of limestone and surrounded by terraced gardens leading down to the riverbanks. Its shutters were the color of saffron rice and faded red designs decorated the door and window facings.

As he drew nearer, Eugene became entranced by the varied colors of the garden and the sunlight glinting off of mirrors that hung from giant shade trees. He found himself transposed to storybook mode. "I am a professional," he reminded himself. "This is not a vacation, this is not a fairy tale." Holding himself with a certain amount of professional restraint and dignity, Eugene knocked on an indigo blue door.

"Come on in!" someone shouted. Eugene walked into a surprisingly spacious living area that opened to a kitchen. He heard Shibu's voice in one of the bedrooms. Like the exterior, the interior radiated. Colorful banners hung from the rafters and instead of furniture, large cushions covered the rug in front of the fireplace. A cat circled his ankles and he bent to pet it. Suddenly, a brown blur shot across the room and flopped onto a plum pillow. He looked up and there stood Shibu in the doorway holding a towel. The brown blur turned out to be a two-year-old girl who screamed with delight and then ran naked through the kitchen and into the garden. "Well, hello!" Shibu greeted him unceremoniously. "You've caught us in the after bath chase." He moved swiftly through the room. "Make yourself at home. I won't be able to give you my complete attention until I put Jasmine down for her nap. Then we can have some tea and chat!" Shibu was already in the garden as he spoke and Eugene heard squeals of laughter before he returned carrying a very dirty little girl who had clearly been rolling in the dirt. "Back in the bath for you, Jasmine!" he laughed, and they disappeared into the other room.

"

Touching means sincerity and connection, in other words, enhancing the level of trust.

"

Chapter 8

Follow Your Intuition and Be Helpful

Eugene took a deep breath and looked around him. The clock said two-thirty. He noticed a row of big and little shoes next to the door. Without a chair, he relied on the wall for support as he removed his new cowboy boots. Might as well stay. Splashing noises and the low murmur of Shibu's voice were the only sounds in the room. Remembering Benjamin's recent advice, Eugene stood still and breathed deeply. Slowly, he padded around the rooms in his socks. Here was an empty basket by the door with a note in it, "14 yellow peppers, 4 green tomatoes", here was a doll on the floor, here was a pile of white linen shirts to be ironed, here was a bowl of batter with a mound of orange rind next to it. Here was an ancient abacus, a Japanese print and a grouping on the mantle of photos. He stopped to inspect a dozen or so pictures. Immediately, his eye fell upon a large photo of Shibu,

Jasmine and another man – Toshi, the House Security Officer. "They must be life partners," he realized with a shock as he inspected the other family photos.

Eugene had scrupulously avoided people who made him uncomfortable. When the subject of homosexuality came up among friends at parties or at the club, he always shrugged and said, "It's none of my business." and he meant it in more ways than one. First, monster trucks and now *this*. Eugene turned away from the photos. Maybe Benjamin could push through these sorts of cultural barriers, but Eugene felt a rush of weariness and a familiar sense of defeat settle in his neck.

He walked to the door and stood staring at the dark blue planks. His left hand swept across something soft and he glanced over at a low bench where he saw a shoeshine kit with felt brushes hanging near the doorpost. He needed to leave. He knew what he had heard about this sort of thing. His hand rested on the soft black felt of the brush. A verse came to his mind, "Whatever your hand finds to do, do it… with all your heart, and do it well, with all sincerity." It was something like that. His intuition propelled him downward and he squatted to inspect the rows of shoes and then finally sat cross-legged on the floor. He chose a tiny pair of brown shoes and began polishing.

Eugene stood up at three o'clock, stretching his back, each shoe in mint condition, if he did say so himself. Shibu and Jasmine had finished their bath and were drawing pictures and cutting with scissors out on the side porch. As four o'clock approached, Eugene had found the tea set, plates, jam and butter and biscuits. His movements were rhythmic and he found himself humming as he washed and dried some dishes. Shibu read Jasmine a story, patted her back until she fell asleep and then he came into the kitchen yawning.

Eugene waved him over to the table, "Have a seat! I hope you don't mind but I took the liberty of preparing our tea." They sat down together at the table and Shibu's glance quickly took in the changes in the house. He faced Eugene.

"

'Whatever your hand finds to do, do it... with all your heart, and do it well, with all sincerity.'

"

Chapter 9

Connections, Comfort and Advocacy

"I don't mind at all, Eugene. Quite the contrary I am grateful."

"Actually," Eugene shrugged, "I've really enjoyed being here, it's been a very relaxing afternoon." He poured the tea serenely. "So, Shibu, tell me about yourself. Where did you go to school, how long have you lived here with Benjamin?"

Shibu laughed. "Well, I received my masters in process engineering at the Sorbonne and my Ph.D. in economics at the London School of Economics, but first, I had to escape my family's rug factory in Veranasi, India...and the young girl they had chosen for me to marry."

Eugene listened carefully and with growing interest. He gleaned from Shibu's casual references to organizations and projects that he stood as a leader in his industry and sat on a number of corporate and charitable boards. Despite his initial and occasional feelings of discomfort about Shibu's life choices, Eugene could not deny a growing sense of identification with this powerful man he had originally seen as merely a house servant. As if Shibu had read his mind, he said, "You know, I wanted a position where I was also of service to others. My parents ran a small rug manufacturing business. All of us worked in the plant and eventually, I was the one who got to go to school. My sisters found positions working in the houses of the upper class. I learned by being with people who were financially successful and from working hard that my privilege is what I make it. I've come to believe over the years that it is a privilege to serve." He put down his tea. "This was delicious. However," he glanced at the clock on the wall, "time is flying and I promised Jasmine I'd make her some chutney. Can I send you back with anything?"

Eugene realized that he had forgotten to ask for what he wanted...again. Surprisingly, he felt awkward asking but he pressed on. "Um. Actually, Shibu, there are two things…I'd like to improve my room in Benjamin's house." Shibu raised his eyebrows.

"What's wrong with your room."

"It seems to be missing quite a few essentials." He looked around him. "While walking to my room I saw other rooms that seemed far more comfortable than where I am." Shibu picked up a silver cell phone,

"Done! Anything else?" Eugene cleared his throat.

"Would you consider being an advocate for me? With your professional contacts, perhaps there are people you know who may need reliable accounting and consulting services." Eugene laid his card on the table.

Shibu picked it up and read it carefully. "I would be happy to recommend you, Eugene, once I've seen your firm's work. Why don't we set up some time to discuss the possibility of some of your services for an overseas concern I manage and then, after a couple of quarters, we'll see about recommending you to my colleagues." Shibu handed Eugene his card. They shook hands warmly, and Eugene passed out of the cottage and into the last hard sun of the day.

"

I learned by being with people who were financially successful and from working hard that my privilege is what I make it. I've come to believe over the years that it is a privilege to serve.

"

"

Wow! How easy was that? I can do this! I can do this. This isn't selling, this is developing relationships.

"

Chapter 10

"Touch" and Ask for What You Want

As he walked back the way he had come along the river, a warm feeling of accomplishment came over Eugene and he consciously added another advocate to his list. Then he remembered, "Ah! I need to call Val back; she can be an advocate for me." He dialed the main ranch number on his cell phone and she picked up right away,

"Hi there, stranger!"

"Hi Val. You know, I wanted to tell you that I really enjoyed our talk earlier. I haven't talked about that sort of stuff, really, ever. It made me think and it also made me realize I miss my wife a lot."

"Yeah? Thanks Eugene, you're sweet to say so."

"Another thing I wanted to do, Val, is ask you for your help."

"Sure."

"I'm an accounting consultant and I'm working at meeting people who have a need for my services in their business. Would you keep me in mind and pass my name along?"

He heard her now familiar little squeal. "Get outta here! You are an accountant? That is *so cool*, Eugene. I never would have taken you for an accountant. You know, the dry, anal-retentive type with little glasses?" She laughed. "My mom, she owns the truck company where, you know, some people buy their trucks to retrofit out for monster truck competitions. I mean she sells the trucks for traditional purposes too, you know. It's a really interesting story how she got where she is. She was an account manager for a trucking company and they were jacking up the prices big time. She had developed such good relationships with her clients that one day she up and starts her own truck supply business and all of those

guys came with her. Cool huh? Anyways, I'm learning the business now for the southern division she
wants to open. I'm kind-of apprenticing, right now,
however, I will be starting next month. Mom told me
I had to go out and procure new services like lawyers,
accountants, and mechanics for down here. She wants
to make some changes anyway. Wow, I'd like to talk
to you more about this Eugene." He heard the phone
ring. "I gotta go! I'll catch you later!"

Eugene turned off his phone. What just happened? He
went over the call in his mind. "Wow, how easy was
that? I can do this! I *can* do this. This isn't selling,
this is developing relationships." He found this first
taste of success intoxicating. "Yeah Baby, bring it on,
I can *handle* it!"

Walking with a swagger he went inside the big house
to get ready for dinner.

"

He wanted to remember the most important lesson of all before Born came through the door: listen.

"

Chapter 11

Listen and Connect

After dinner, Benjamin led him to his room. This time, it was a different room. As Eugene pushed open a large carved door, the sound of a fountain met his ears. The soft glow of stars filtered through French doors leading to a patio. A room lay before him rich in textures, colors and exotic art. A small but eclectic library glowed in the light of an old white lamp. A massage table stood ready and the subtle scent of magnolias wafted in from the tree outside.

"I see that you asked for what you wanted and needed," Benjamin observed with a wink as he said good night.

Eugene woke up the next morning with one thought on his mind: research. If he was going to work with Val and Shibu, he had to know about their companies

71

inside and out. Unfortunately, the one thing he had not asked for was a computer and an Internet connection. Looking on the list of staff members, he identified Born as the person in charge of hardware and software. With confidence now, he dialed zero.

"Hi Eugene! I'm looking forward to our meeting tomorrow."

"Me too, Val. Say, I wanted to talk to Born. I understand that he's in charge of hardware and software. Val is there any thing you can tell me about Born, such as his likes and dislikes, or where he is from, so I can get to know him a little better?

"Hmm. I know he's fluent in Spanish. He's very into all things Latino from what I can tell."

"Really? Well, that's interesting."

"I'll go ahead and connect you, OK.?"

"Thanks Val."

Eugene was rather proud of his own Spanish and decided to try some of it out on Born if the opportunity arose. He dialed Born's number and a very quiet voice answered the phone. Eugene remembered a pale, blond man of medium height. The small talk he had intended to make evaporated and he found himself flustered and simply blurting out what he needed within the first few minutes.

"Certainly, I will be up in half an hour to hook you up," Born responded helpfully and just as the two men were about to hang up Eugene blurted out,

"I understand that you're a student of the Spanish or Latin culture!" He continued hurriedly, "Do you salsa?"

"Do you mean salsa dance?" Born laughed modestly. "Yes, I do actually. Do you?"

"I'm embarrassed to try it now, but I dated a woman from Panama for a while before I met my wife and we used to go salsa dancing all the time. I also learned how to meranga and mamba as well. I heard you spoke Spanish and I wondered if you knew of a spot where I might brush up on my dancing in the city. My wife wants to go dancing."

"I know of a few places. I also teach it myself here at the house gym for Benjamin and some of the staff. You're welcome to join in. We have a class tonight."

When he got off of the phone with Born, Eugene felt as if he had just single-handedly invented the science of building relationship skills. Who knew what surprises his relationship with Born held? He did know the importance of making a connection, asking for what he wanted and staying with the defined processes Benjamin had revealed to him.

In less than thirty minutes he would have an opportunity to practice what he'd learned as he interacted with Born. Standing still in his beautiful room, Eugene closed his eyes and listened to the small sounds around him. He heard water bubbling in the fountain, birds, a vacuum cleaner running, a gate creaking open, hooves moving and laughter.

He wanted to remember the most important lesson of all before Born came through the door: listen.

"

Eugene was beside himself. He loved trap doors and secret openings. Hoping to catch Born up in a conversation, he peppered him with questions about other such imaginative constructions in the house.

"

Chapter 12

Is Failure an Option?

At the light knock on his door, Eugene opened it to find himself looking into a pair of pale blue eyes.

Born's appearance was as unassuming as his manner. Eugene realized that he had expected to meet a man in an open white shirt, tight Euro jeans and pointed Spanish shoes. Born's tennis shoes peeked out from the hems of his too big jeans. His shirt, a collarless knit in dull green also looked baggy on him.

Born shook hands briefly and wheeled his computer cart with a CPU, keyboard, monitor and other equipment on it into the room. Eugene realized that the room lacked a desk.

"I'm not sure where we're going to put that," he said following Born into the room. With the barest smile,

Born tossed his hair out of his eyes and began scrutinizing the section of wall opposite Eugene's bed next to the fireplace.

"Ah, here it is!" He muttered and pressed with his index finger on a nearly imperceptible rise in the plaster. With a single click, a six-foot section of wall began to move. Eugene watched with amazement as a desk and chair with all the necessary connections pivoted into view.

"Magic! Wow!" Eugene was beside himself. He loved trap doors and secret openings. Hoping to catch Born up in a conversation, he peppered him with questions about other such imaginative constructions in the house. Finally, Born chuckled.

"I'm just the software/hardware guy. You need to ask Benjamin these questions. He designed the house." Born went to work setting up the computer. He was not a big talker and after learning about his passion for Latin culture in clipped sentences, Eugene settled back in an armchair feeling a bit like a pest. He shook off an old feeling of frustration.

"So…Born, I've noticed that several of the staff members have their own business concerns. Are you among them?" After a short pause as he typed onto the screen command line, Born replied,

"Um, yes. I own a currency brokerage firm in Uruguay I'm here for several months to set up a banking relationship in the states." Eugene blinked.

"Oh, how interesting." He began to cast about in his mind for comments or questions, though he was quite frankly shocked by this new information, he still wanted to say something pertinent about the currency exchange business. Just then Born stood up and began wrapping a spare cable around his hand and elbow.

"You're ready, Eugene." Without ado, Born pushed his cart to the door and opened it.

"Let me know if you have any problems." Eugene rose to his feet in dismay. That was so fast it was mind-boggling! Born was walking out the door and Eugene hadn't made a meaningful connection with him!

"Thanks a lot Born. I'll see you at the salsa class tonight."

Born nodded, "Yes, come! The women will be glad to have a new partner." He smiled and with an efficient turn, began wheeling his cart down the hall. Eugene looked around his beautiful room with his new computer in it.

"What just happened here?" he asked himself with dismay. "I listened, I talked but somehow…somehow nothing happened." He sat down at the desk and absently logged onto the Internet. Even as the familiar sights of cyberspace greeted him, Eugene fought off a sense of defeat. "I'll talk to Benjamin about this." He promised himself. With that, he tried to put his failed connection with Born out of his mind.

"

I listened, I talked but somehow...somehow nothing happened.

"

"

I like to say that you have to listen people into buying. To do that you need to establish an agenda for what you're going to discuss; very much like finding the right rhythm!

"

Chapter 13

Establish an Agenda Early

When Eugene stepped into the gym, the smell of
roasting meat and something that smelled like apples
and cinnamon wrapped around his head. In the corner
opposite from the food a group of musicians were
warming up. This, he realized, was much more than a
dance lesson. This was a real party.

As if on cue, the rest of the staff began arriving at
seven o'clock on the dot. Benjamin came in the back
door and spoke briefly to the cooks before walking
over to the musicians, which included a keyboard
player, a guitarist, a drummer and a horn player.
Eugene mentioned the tall bongo drums to Benjamin
when the old man approached him.

"Oh yes." Benjamin smiled. "There are many dances
one cannot do without a good drum. For instance,

often in Haitian dance, each woman takes a turn letting her hips flirt with the drums." Benjamin winked. "Ah! I love music! This band can really play – just wait!"

"I can see that the stage is set for fun." Eugene said. The room filled with people and the band began to play a melodic old tune.

"Do you recognize this?" Benjamin asked him. Eugene cocked his head to one side.

"Yes…I think I do. Isn't that *Just the Way You Look Tonight*?" Benjamin nodded and began softly singing along,

"Someday when I'm awfully low, when the world is cold, I will feel a glow just thinking of you…and the way you look tonight." He hummed a few more bars. "That song works so well, do you know why?" Eugene thought for a minute,

"It seems to just roll off of your tongue. It's so easy to sing, like a scale."

"Right. Jerome Kern wrote the music and he made the song work just like a scale. Melodies where you don't have to skip around on the scale make you want to sing along don't they?" He continued to hum and sway, clearly in his element.

Born, clad in shiny Spanish shoes and well-tailored black pants, walked past Eugene on his way to the front of the room.

"Hi there Born!" Eugene called out to him. Born looked up and smiled and waved to Eugene, his face registering that he could not quite place him at the moment. Eugene's heart sank in defeat.

Born took his place in the front of the room to begin the salsa lesson. Eugene bent closer to Benjamin's ear.

"Benjamin, could I have a conversation with you later?" Benjamin nodded while his eyes eagerly took in everything around him. He was clearly relishing every moment. He shot a penetrating look at Eugene.

"Yes, I made sure that I would be free to talk with

you this evening."

Jostling and laughing as he switched partners every ten minutes or so, Eugene began to formulate the exact question he wanted to ask Benjamin. An hour and many turns later, Eugene sat down at one of the long tables with a plate of aromatic South American delicacies.

The band moved into North Brazilian folk music while people ate and then followed that with some old big band era favorites. After a bout of salsa, the band settled for the rest of evening into mostly American jazz. Benjamin sat down next to Eugene. He had been dancing with several women and looked a little worn out. With little ado, he drank a large glass of water and said, "What's on your mind, Eugene?"

Eugene cleared his throat nervously. "Well, Benjamin, after talking with Born earlier today, I realized that just trying to listen might be good enough for some people, but it's not an adequate way to approach everyone. It occurred to me that since listening is so integral to winning new clients, you might just have a process for that as well." He stopped, took a deep breath and shot a glance in Benjamin's direction.

"You deduced correctly, my friend. I like the way you're figuring me out!" The band struck up a swing tune by Louis Armstrong. "Do you remember how I described the great song, *Just The Way You Look Tonight*?"

Eugene nodded, "A melody close to the scale."

"That's right. Listening is like making music. In the beginning of a relationship you need a form, like a scale, to follow." Benjamin's bright eyes crinkled up around the corners as he concentrated. "I like to say that you have to listen people into buying. To do that you need to establish an agenda for what you're going to discuss; very much like finding the right rhythm! Are you with me?" Eugene nodded, his eyes wide as he tried to drink in Benjamin's words. Benjamin pushed a few napkins and a pen toward him. "Don't be afraid to take notes when you're listening to someone. People like to know that you want to keep their words. So, where was I? Oh yes, agenda.

"Once you've established a connection, taken the time to find out what is important to your client, (which I think you now know how to do), your second step is to find out about your client's business. Now, I know that with several people whom you've met here the information about what they do and what you have to offer has risen rather naturally to the surface, and I'm saying that that isn't a response you can count on.

"Take Born, for instance. Once you found out about him and his interests were you able to discover that he owns a currency brokerage in Uruguay?"

"Yes. I did find that out about Born, but then things just sort-of fizzled out. I did spend a lot of time asking him questions about trap doors and secret passageways in the house." Eugene admitted. The band broke into the Beatles' song, *You've Got to Hide Your Love Away*.

"Don't feel too bad." Benjamin said, "Most new sales people talk a lot about themselves, what they have to offer or, in your case, what you happen to find interesting. Remember, your goal is to live in your potential client's space, find their rhythm, work in their space and then move on. Too often professionals looking for new clients never leave their own space, talking about who they are and what they can do for the client. It sounds to me like you even weakened the connection that you did have with Born."

Eugene gulped. "I guess I did."

Benjamin continued, "Things fizzled out with Born because you did not bring a listening agenda with you. Now, after you've made a connection and discovered what kind of business someone does, the third piece of information you want to discover is what sort of needs they may have. Step three is where you really have to be precise in your listening." The band moved into an easy swing song and Benjamin began clapping along.

"Step three is like the bridge of a song, Eugene. It's that transition that brings body and interest to the verse and chorus. Ba bob, ba bob, oh dippity de de de dummm." Benjamin drummed the table with his fingertips.

"We need to find out three things from the potential client to identify their true needs: Identify their personal fears, discover their unique vision for their business and finally uncover the values that drive their decisions. I call this PFV^2 (V squared). Basically," Benjamin continued, "determining someone's personal fears, vision and values allows you to tap into their true needs. PFV^2 = Needs."

Eugene looked up from his notes quizzically. "So I just get down and ask them key questions like, 'What are your needs?'"

Benjamin chuckled, "First, I allow them to talk about themselves and their business. Let's take Born again. If I were talking with him I'd say, 'A currency brokerage in Uruguay? That's interesting. How did you get started in that line of work? Or, that sounds like an exciting business these days. How did you get started in that line of business? Then, I'd shut up and listen! Listen for the "magic music" to come from them as they describe their passion. After I listen to him for a while, making mental notes, I'd make my big move. And that's to get an opportunity to sit down and discuss the possibilities to do work together. I'd say something like, 'Born, I'd like to find out more about you and your business and then share with you some of the things my firm is doing as we partner with organizations such as yours. Can we set up some time to talk further?' Notice that I didn't try to act as if I know his business. Setting up a future meeting allows you to do your homework. After doing research, you can make the necessary connection point where you can be of service to their company. I would then say, 'What works best for you, mornings or afternoons?'

"Either way, by asking specific questions I've given him a jumping off place for talking to me."

"Whew!" Eugene exclaimed, laying down his pen. " I get it Benjamin. You're really uncovering the nuts and bolts for me." Just then, Yi, the House Electronics Manager stepped up to Eugene. She had short salt and pepper hair and dragon earrings bobbing from her ears.

"Eugene, would you like to dance?" The tune was fairly fast paced.

Benjamin patted him on the shoulder, "You go ahead. I'll be here when you get back."

As Eugene stepped out on the dance floor, he realized where he had seen Yi before. She was the woman who had greeted him at the gate riding the black stallion. He remembered how anxious and unsure of himself he'd been when he first saw her. She laughed and spun from his arms gracefully. Eugene watched himself dancing with Yi in amazement. He felt his personal power rise up like a symphonic roar of joy and relief. His feet moved nimbly. He lifted their arms up high like a canopy and twirled her, then himself under it.

"

'Basically,' Benjamin continued, 'determining someone's personal fears, vision and values allows you to tap into their true needs. PFV^2 = Needs.'

"

"

Watch and listen to learn what someone's values are. Look for things that they surround themselves with like family, trophies or pictures. I have found that by asking what they do in their spare time often taps into their values.

"

Chapter 14

Connecting to their Rhythm and Passion

When Eugene came back to the table Benjamin clapped. "Well done!"

"I'll see you at breakfast tomorrow." Yi called as she walked away.

"She's awesome! She builds electric guitars and knows a ton of musicians!" Eugene felt like he had never had so much fun.

"Are you ready to hear about the V squared?" Benjamin brought him back to their conversation.

"Yes!" Do you mean their vision for their successes, their goals for the future and what they value the most?"

"I do. Again, now you've had a chance to do your homework. Paraphrase what you had talked about before and then ask specific questions to get your potential client talking again. After finding out more about their operation, I'd say something like, 'What have been some of the high points for you?'

'What would you like to see your business become ultimately?' As for his or her values, these belong in every word and movement. Watch and listen to learn what someone's values are. Look for things that they surround themselves with like family, trophies or pictures. I have found that by asking what they do in their spare time often taps into their values.

"You know, Eugene, learning about these needs, fears, visions and values of a potential customer puts you in the position to offer them something they really need. People's fears can tell us if we have something to offer them, a solution to those fears. Maybe there's something that is keeping them awake at night. Whatever their fears are, they will tell you once they trust you and that leads to your next step: Determining whether or not there is a marriage between what the potential client is looking for and the services we, or specifically you and your firm, provide.

"If the answer to that question is *yes* then you can ask your potential client, 'What will it take for us to move toward doing business together." Benjamin finished.

Eugene relaxed his shoulders and leaned back in his chair. "It's the tools, the processes that you've given me Benjamin that make such a difference. I can understand systems," he said more quietly, almost to himself.

Benjamin put both of his hands on the table and got ready to stand up. "Make no mistake, young man, these systems are good; they're great, even; and it's like the difference between jazz before Louis Armstrong and the jazz after Louis Armstrong. He brought something to the music that you can't write down, something that is only passed down by listening and resides in his soul. It's rhythmic improvisation. It's a feeling, a swing somewhere in between the things you can measure and where you can only imagine. In the end, it's whether or not you really care about these people you want to be your clients that allows you to make that sweet rain. Like music, finding that right rhythm with a potential client is when the rain finally comes your way."

It's a feeling, a swing somewhere in between the things you can measure. In the end, it's whether or not you really care about these people you want to be your clients...

"

Eugene felt intuitively that this would be a good time to let Yi know that he was listening to her by summarizing what he had heard so far.

"

Chapter 15

One Step at a Time

At seven-thirty the next morning Eugene met Yi in the rose garden. He had to follow a circuitous route through paths to find the lush hideaway. Yi sat at a stone table against a backdrop of wild roses climbing the wall behind her. The table was set with breads, fruits and fresh juice and coffee.

They greeted each other warmly and Eugene, careful to build on the connection that he had made the night before while getting to know her and adhering to his discovery agenda, remarked,

"What a beautiful setting! It reminds me of a Hawaiian scene. You mentioned that you live in Hawaii."

"Yes, my husband and I were both born in Hong Kong and we moved to Hawaii almost thirty years ago." Yi shared.

"Do you have these types of roses in Hawaii?" Eugene asked as he bent to smell a giant white blossom.

"Yes and no. Of course anything grows in Hawaii, though these sorts of roses are not native to the islands. It is the same luxurious effect of Hawaii that I like, though."

Eugene sat across from her and took a quick sip of the hot coffee. "Mmm. Perfect.

So, tell me more about you and your husband, Yi. Is he a musician?"

Yi smiled shyly, "No, Al teaches computer science at the University of Hawaii."

"Al? Is that a Chinese name?"

"Well, yes and no. We both went to Catholic schools. The nuns gave him the name Aloysius after a saint. They named me Amy. I prefer to use my Chinese name, Yi, but Al has stayed with his English name."

"So Yi, you mentioned several well-known musicians to me. How did you get to know so many musicians?"

She laughed shyly, obviously enjoying Eugene's enthusiasm. Without answering him directly, she asked, "Well, tell me, what sort of music do you like, Eugene?"

"Jazz mostly, but I really enjoy most music."

"Hmm. Have you ever heard of Peter White?"

"Peter White!?" Eugene could barely contain himself. "He's one of my favorites! I really like him and Dave Koz."

Yi nodded knowingly. "You are a very romantic man, then. They are both romantic jazz musicians. I have met Peter and he is a wonderful person, though I'm not saying that he has bought guitars from me. I have not met David yet, but when I do, I will tell him I know a fan of his."

Eugene felt buzzed with the talk about what he loved and he had to make an effort to step back and redirect the conversation toward Yi and her business.

"Yi, wasn't there a famous electric guitar made in Hawaii?" Yi looked impressed.

"Well, actually, solid body electric guitars were inspired by the metal slide guitars in the '20s and '30s in Hawaii." She looked at him quizzically, "You know electric guitar talk is a lot of Fender, Gibson, coil and magnet. Are you really up for that?" Eugene laughed and buttered a cranberry orange muffin.

"You know, Yi, I do find the industry fascinating. What I'd really like to know is more about how you got started in your business. For instance, how long have you been operating, what have been the peaks and valleys so far?" Yi put down her coffee cup and appraised Eugene.

"Well, I can tell you that I own a very old company with an excellent reputation. We have customers from all over the world. I am proud of our craftsmanship. My goal has been to work with the electromagnetic pieces of the guitar to give it a longer life. Right now, our guitars "die" or the coils stop polarizing to the magnets after about four or five years. I am experimenting with unconventional types of insulation." She looked down and stirred her yogurt pensively. "I have another goal, but it is more personal."

"Tell me please."

Yi looked up carefully. "You can see, Eugene, I am a pretty assertive, outspoken woman. You may not know this, but assertive Asian-born women are not that common. I came from Hong Kong and actually earned a Masters in psychology before I went into electrical engineering. I have a passion to teach other Asian-born women to speak up for themselves and learn assertiveness." Eugene raised his eyebrows.

105

"So, on top of maintaining an enviable position in a highly competitive industry, you also want to change the way many Asian women interact with the world?" Yi gave him her first wide smile.

"You are perceptive! That is what I am trying to do exactly. All of my guitars are made by hand. You know, machines are limited and cannot produce the kind of imperfections into the craft that make a good guitar. I struggle with this idea all of the time. The Asian women I've trained as crafts people are mostly from Communist China. They cannot accept imperfection as a positive thing.

"Our woods are not specific. I choose those that I sense harbor beauty or music within them." She laughed. "Many people call me crazy but I sell the best for the best prices."

Eugene nodded. "Say, Yi, do you mind if I write some of this down? I don't want to forget it."

Very politely, Yi nodded, "Please, feel free."

Eugene felt intuitively that this would be a good time to let Yi know that he was listening to her by summarizing what he had heard so far. "So, would I be way off if I said that it sounds like one of the fears you may have surrounding your business right now is the effectiveness of your labor force and possibly another fear is that you would not be the first to make the newest electromagnetic innovations, that someone else will beat you to it?"

Yi pondered his statement. "*Fear* is an interesting word. I suppose that it is accurate. My women are the key to keeping the craft alive. Yet, I struggle with them everyday. Let me tell you a story to illustrate this. Just last week, I had a bouquet of flowers in my hands. Our shop is full of drills and saws. I like to keep the beauty of the natural world present. I handed the flowers to one of my newly arrived intern workers, Wendy, and asked her to choose a vase and put them in it. She stood holding the flowers and looking at me helplessly. There were five vases of varying sizes in front of her. 'I can't.' she said to me. 'Please tell me which vase.' I said, 'Just try to make a decision on your own and I will support you.' I could see

107

that it was very difficult for her to make a choice without a directive. You see, in Communist China, one mistake could cost you a lifetime of suffering, so independent thought cannot exist. A few minutes later, I looked over to see the bouquet of flowers stuffed into a vase much too small for it.

"Wendy, I said, 'You made a decision, you found a vase for the flowers. Wonderful! Good job! Now, I would like to ask you a question about your choice, why did you chose such a small vase?' Do you know what she told me? She told me that she did not want to waste water! It is very frustrating for me, Eugene, but I stayed patient with her and suggested that the next time she weigh the risk of using more water or making the flowers unattractive in too small of a vase. You can see the kind of challenge I have to train these women to create unique and world-class guitars. I would like to spend more time working with them, but I must also be in the electronic lab as well as buying wood." She paused, gauging his interest and decided to continue.

"It is not just about making good electric guitars for me, Eugene. It is about redeeming the potential of women I care about. Assertiveness and thinking skills can mean the difference between abuse or invisibility and a life of kindness and affluence for any person - especially women." She stopped, clearly afraid that she had told him more than he cared to hear.

Eugene sensed Yi's insecurity and sought to reassure her of his interest. "It sounds to me as if you are running a school for assertiveness training within the context of making electric guitars. I can see how that would put a strain on your business focus, yet provide you with long-term satisfaction."

Yi's eyes widened and she looked at him incredulously. "You read my mind! I have been toying with the idea of setting up a separate entity, like a school or an Asian culture center for a long time. I am not sure how it would fly…financially though."

Surprised that he had stumbled upon her idea of a school, Eugene decided to recap again what he had heard Yi say. A practice he and Rozlyn had developed during their courtship was to repeat back to the other party what they had heard before proceeding with any of their own conclusions. This made the other person feel heard, which Eugene suddenly realized, was the crux not only of marriage but also of business relationships.

"Can I tell you what I've heard you say to me so far?" Yi nodded. "I've heard you point out that your company is one of the top in its field of crafting handmade electric guitars. You have somewhat unconventional methods that make your guitars better than those made by machines. Your client base is international and elite. To stay on top of the market, you are researching ways to improve electromagnetic pickup on your guitars. In the shop, you have brought in women from Communist China and trained them as guitar makers. This fulfills your labor need and your desire to improve the lives of Asian women. You find yourself increasingly pulled in two directions, however and you would like to find a way to address your passion for teaching assertiveness skills without compromising your electric guitar manufacturing business."

"Yes, Eugene. That is what I said. You are a good listener." Yi paused and with careful politeness asked, "Do you think that your firm might be able to help me structure such a school financially?" She sighed. "I cannot do this by myself."

Eugene leaned forward slightly, "I think that we could find a way to structure your business into a couple of entities to satisfy both of your goals without negatively impacting the other."

Yi's face brightened. She looked as if a weight had been lifted from her and she radiated hope. "Really? Eugene, of course I am cautious, but I would very much like to meet with you and see what we can do to make this a reality."

Eugene felt strangely calm. "I know we can help you, Yi. At the next meeting, you and I will go over a specific needs analysis." He poured more coffee into his cup and reached out to pull a rose to his face. "These are so lovely." Smiling inside, he breathed deeply of its perfume and let the joy of being alive seep into his pores.

The time commitment to making his marketing a success meant that he would have to delegate some of his technical project management responsibilities to other people on his team.

Chapter 16

Make Time Commitments and Make Them Work

As he strolled back to his room, Eugene went over in his mind what Benjamin had taught him the night before. PFV^2 means that, Personal Fears, Visions and Values equal one's needs. Yi certainly had all of these things and she had expressed them to him with candor.

Carefully, Eugene recalled how Yi had consistently gauged him for listening interest before continuing. "She was careful not to tell me more than I wanted to hear. If I had not been truly engaged with her; if I had become preoccupied with my favorite musicians for instance, she would not have revealed her real fears and needs to me." He could see now that once he had laid a foundation of discovery and research, closing an account did not take a lot of sales know-how.

113

Replaying the conversation over and over in his head, Eugene realized that Benjamin had given him a priceless tool. In one corner of the garden, he saw the stooped back of a gardener among giant lavender bushes.

Pulled from his reverie he began to notice that the paths and terraces around him had been put together with great forethought. The combination of silvers and greens rose up to merge with spectacular spider orange and that was crowned with floating seas of white-feathered plants. Nearby, dark hibiscus leaves broke into fuchsia blooms and orchids floated near a tiny waterfall.

Every section of the garden was planned, tended and left to become a natural masterpiece. Suddenly, Eugene felt suffused in emotion. His chest tightened and he swallowed hard. Reaching into his pocket, he pulled out his cell phone and dialed Rozlyn's number. He had kept in touch with his wife every evening, but now he felt the need to hear her voice.

"Hello?"

"Hi Sweetheart."

"What a nice surprise! How are you?"

"I'm good. I…I just wanted to hear your voice. Roz, I've learned so much these past few days and not just about selling accounting services."

"Tell me about it."

"Oh, Roz, there's so much to tell, but right now, I just wanted to say that I love you and I realize that there's so much about you that I still need to discover."

Rozlyn murmured in a pleased voice, "I love you too, Honey. When are you coming home?"

"The day after tomorrow ."

"OK., Eugene. I'll see you soon."

"Love You."

"Love you, too. Bye."

Eugene clicked his phone off and opened the door to his room. He'd come a long way from the empty room with the bare mattress and the heavy, black rotary phone. He remembered dialing zero in desperation and hearing Val's voice spring back at him. This had not been an easy journey and he suspected that once he left Benjamin's house and went out into the world, he would encounter even more frustrations.

He ran over the equations in his mind,

$$(TA + CRS + PA) \times AD = Success, \text{ and}$$

$$(80/20)\ 16\ (m^3).$$

Sitting down at his desk, Eugene worked for the next five hours to create a varied marketing plan that allowed him to "touch" each of his advocate clients sixteen times a year. He then created a list of people and organizations that he planned to tap as master-mind-mentoring groups. This proved to be difficult for him. He realized that he would have to proffer invitations to a number of people and work at gathering the kind of support group he needed around him.

Building a structure was not going to be easy, he knew that. He looked up again at the equations he had jotted down at the top of his legal pad. Achievement drive: that's what he had to sustain and, he stubbornly dug his mental heels in, that is what he had. He'd comb the city and beyond to find the right combination of people to give him the dynamic interaction he needed to build a solid mastermind network.

Finally, Eugene completed the thorough research he had begun on the trucking industries and Val's business in particular. He reread the information on Shibu's various concerns that he had compiled and printed it out, making a note to check on the shipping and exchange rates for manufactured goods coming from India to the United States.

The time commitment to making his marketing a success meant that he would have to delegate some of his technical project management responsibilities to other people on his team. Not wanting to lose his momentum, Eugene created a spreadsheet of various jobs, skill sets and employees. He carefully noted each person's current commitments and worked to dovetail new responsibilities into what they were already doing.

The job of synchronizing his schedule to fit in his current job with his marketing activities strained even Eugene's analytical mind. Several times, he got up and paced the room, stood before the fountain and breathed deeply.

Benjamin's voice came to him saying, "Where we spend our time and talent is a reflection of what is most important to us."

"If I want to do this, I can create the time and the space for it to happen." He told himself and went back to the desk. Taking his hard-won control and relinquishing it to juniors was tough on his ego. "There's more stretching involved in this than just accommodating different types of people," Eugene gritted his teeth and pushed forward, determined to have a plan in hand when he returned to the office.

The thought then crossed his mind, "Whom should I

mentor?" Now that he had learned so much from Benjamin, he knew he must pass it on. He went over his team members again in his mind, thinking of each of them. Who would step forward with the desire and the drive to become the next manager on the path to becoming a partner? Perhaps it would be someone outside of his firm in the community that he and Rozlyn were continually growing around them. Eugene had never really mentored anyone else before and Benjamin hadn't really discussed this skill with him. At the same time, Benjamin had shown him how day after day.

Eugene made notes about his own mentoring experience with Benjamin. Under the word *Mentoring* he wrote:

1) Get a commitment for change.
2) Go slow!
3) Make them work to learn their lessons, don't give them away.
4) Tell stories.
5) Make it fun.
6) Allow people to learn from their failures.
7) Listen.

8) Remember each person is unique, don't expect one to be like the other.

As the sun began to cast shadows in the trees beyond his windows, Eugene rose to get ready for dinner. He was looking forward to leaving and he hated to go at the same time.

He knotted his tie and found himself humming an old Gladys Knight and the Pips song,

"Yeah, hmm, yeah
Do you know that some folks know about it, some don't.
Some will learn to shout it, some won't.
But sooner or later baby, here's a ditty,
Say you're gonna have to get right down to the real nitty gritty.
hmm, hmm, hmm.

Come on and let the good times roll
Let the music sink down in to your soul
hmm, hmm

You gotta get right down to the really nitty gritty
Get on down, get on down."

Eugene danced his way down the big spiral staircase, the smell of good food and the promise of good conversation minutes away.

"

Where we spend our time and talents is a reflection of what is most important to us.

"

Chapter 17

Pay It Forward: Mentor

Eugene spent the next day introducing himself to a few more staff members, meeting with Val and Shibu, grooming the roan and walking with Benjamin by the river.

Eugene's fortunes had changed forever. Material wealth seemed less important yet it felt as though it was about to flow to him now. Despite this, he continued to resist the differences he encountered in other people. It was in his discovery of a new way of approaching those differences that Eugene found his greatest feeling of success. Each time he connected with a new person, he felt a sense of mastery like none he had ever known. "Taking the time to find out what is important to other people may truly be the secret to connecting," he concluded.

On his last night, he stood out on his patio looking at the stars. The wind blew the limbs of the magnolia tree and the white blooms moved. From the darkness an unfamiliar and yet, familiar accent fell on his ear. The voice was faint. "The night is when Africa wakes up! Crocodiles, big cats and the trickster spider come alive in the African night." Eugene strained his eyes, but all he could see was the outline of a pale shirt near the tree.

"Who are you?"

The man stood without speaking, and Eugene waited. Finally, he heard the rich voice say firmly, "I am ready to say good-bye, my friend."

Eugene's eyes had adjusted to the dark. He began to walk toward the figure, thinking it was perhaps the gardener he had seen a couple of days before.

"Sir, do you know Benjamin? Are you the one who told him about keeping the silver from between him and the marketplace?"

"Benjamin? Yes, I know him well. No, my friend, that story was given to Benjamin by a mentor when he was a young man. I want you to promise that you, too will give it to other young men and women after they discover the courage to ask for guidance."

Eugene approached the figure. "I promise." An old man stepped from the deep recesses with open arms and hugged Eugene. The old man's arms were thin and he felt as light as a feather to Eugene. They looked into each other's eyes. "Benjamin!" With a nod and a smile, Benjamin slowly turned and began to walk away, striking up a song as he went.

Eugene watched him go, mesmerized by the melodic chant in an African language, wondering when they'd meet again…then trying to catch hold of the song Benjamin was singing. As the cadence faded into the trees it sounded to him like one person calling and another person answering. Though he did not understand the meaning of the words, Eugene realized that in his heart of hearts, he knew the song: It was one of joy, intrigue and of course, a message.

"

'I want you to promise that you, too will give it to other young men and women after they discover the courage to ask for guidance.'

"

Ed's Keynotes

The Rainmaker's Strategies for Success

Successful salespeople learn how to multiply their efforts and develop managers into rainmakers. Combine dynamite selling strategies with transformative training and create a succession plan that allows you to retire early.

4 Giant Steps to Leadership

Uncover your own meaning of success and powerful ways of being. The extraordinary gifts of role models illuminate valuable roads to integrity, clarity and ultimately strong personal leadership.

From Fighting the Storm to Dancing in the Rain: Managing Change

Change: make it work for you! Shifts in your organization and industry are inevitable. Learn to revel in the opportunity of the unknown and embrace, not resist, possibility for your professional future.

Ed's Seminars

<u>The Rainmaker's Strategies for Success</u>

Choose from 15 different modules of client development skills to design a structured process for developing long-term business relationships. A variety of interactive exercises and discussions prepares participants to walk away with a practical and usable process ready for implementation.

<u>Team Building and Advanced Coaching</u>

Leaders of today must accomplish more goals with greater results at a faster pace than ever before. In doing so, the leader is called upon to set and maintain a climate within the work group that encourages others to produce. Setting this climate and encouraging others involves High Performance Coaching skills.

<u>The Power of Influencing the Team</u>

Influencing others through interaction and collaboration requires strong communication skills and strategies. This highly-interactive program assists participants in identifying communication and behavioral styles. Participants learn how to work with others to integrate ideas and create within their organization a respectful, collaborative and productive environment.

The Change Train: Get on Board!

Change is guaranteed; progress is not. Technology solves many technical concerns and often creates more. Our role as professionals must evolve to keep pace with the changes in this world. This program focuses on ways to cope, survive, and thrive through the myriad changes we experience everyday. It brings practical suggestions to ensure that as the roles change, value is added to the organization.

Work, Life, Balance and Prioritization

Are you driven by your career? Do you often find yourself not making time for the personal relationship in your life? By developing and sharing strategies to alleviate the varied demands on your time, you will learn how to enjoyably get the right things done, at the right time, for the right reasons.

Ready, Aim Fire!
How to Refocus your Projects

This presentation is designed to provide a "big picture" understanding of the essentials of project team success. The program models up to twelve skills and attributes critical to effective project management.

Ed's Order Form

Becomming aRainmaker Manual

    Send me_____ x $89.85 = _____

Life's Lessons That Create Leaders CD

    Send me_____ x $14.85 = _____

4 Giant Steps to Leadership Book

    Send me_____ x $14.85 = _____

Work/Life Balance Workbook and Video CD

    Send me_____ x $50.00 = _____

Teambuilding and Advanced Coaching Workbook

    Send me_____ x $35.85 = _____

Conflict Resolution and Dealing with Difficult Behaviors Workbook

    Send me_____ x $35.85 = _____

DISC Behavioral Profile with Coaching Option

    Send me_____ x $75.00 = _____

Ed's fax--->   **210-342-4822**

Mail --->   **Advanced Marketing Concepts**
                    7 Royal Waters Drive
                    San Antonio, TX 78248

Call --->   1-800-381-1433

Email--->   ed@edspeaks.com

For more information on Ed Robinson
seminars, books and CDs

**Ed Robinson
Advanced Marketing
Concepts, Inc.
7 Royal Waters Drive
San Antonio, TX 78248
1-800-381-1433
210-342-4866
Email: ed@edspeaks.com
www.edspeaks.com**